THE LOOTERS

THE LOOTERS

Robert Minhinnick

SEREN BOOKS
*1989

SEREN BOOKS is the book imprint of
Poetry Wales Press Ltd
Andmar House, Tondu Road, Bridgend
Mid Glamorgan

British Library Cataloguing in Publication Data

Minhinnick, Robert, 1952-
The looters
I. Title
823'.914

ISBN 1-85411-019-5

Cover Painting: Detail from 'Our World' by Diana Evans

*The publisher acknowledges the financial support of the
Welsh Arts Council*

Typeset in 11 point Palatino by Megaron, Cardiff
Printed by John Penry Press, Swansea

Contents

ANTS

(For Australia in 1988, on its 'Bicentennial')

In the bar you watched the miners
Try to drink the uranium
Out of their bellies, each frayed
Green page of the bankroll
Waved like a new discovery.

Behind the backdoor in the yard
Are the grey-haired men and women
Rubbing their misshapen dugs,
The still uncertain tight-browed boys
Finally tearing the ringpulls

From the fizzing cans, spilling
Oblivion over the grass
As a tribe of worker-ants appear
And roll the sweetened crumbs of earth
Back to their pavilions.

Perhaps it was your skin, the colour
Of their bootsoles, those men didn't like.
But they too are as dark as the cliff's
Obsidian the company's
Impatient dynamite reveals.

What they could not understand
Was not being able to ticket you
With one of the street's natural
Felonies, those predictably
Contagious lusts

That fill one side in the notebook,
Especially when the sand, storm-whipped,
Rattles the beerhouse walls
And spins in a ragged helix
About the edge of town,

Its grains swarming
Around the neon bulbs
Like ants on desert orchids.
But your behaviour they could tell
Was no bad weather incivility.

Your people once walked
Down the spine of a continent,
Discovering the one right name
For the lizard, the right name for the tree,
Laying the highway with their songs.

Now your father swats at daylight
In his corral of cans,
Sometimes pushing a broom for a dollar
Around the trailer-park.
He is the chief who serves at the diesel-pump,

Magician without a memory,
Watching and offering no comment
As the young men suck the whisky stem,
Then pour gasoline
Over the ant-thrones. In the dark

They whisper like phosphorous,
Those beacons that once had names,
The hot, red kilns where a people
Unmakes itself. Vivid as a cave-
Painting, each gallery turns to flame.

The meagre room they put you in
Has a bucket and a striped pillow,
The graffiti-scrawl of insect-blood.
You're drunk on words, the gaoler says,
That newspaper talk about rights.

At dawn the men in yellow trucks
Burrow across their mooncrater,
A hole to lose this township in.
Around the shacks your dogs still sleep,
And if there's an absence

No-one speaks of a drinking-place unfilled
Or a gap in the welfare line.
So many of your sort might not appear
For days or weeks before the slow
Perplexed acknowledgement of wrong.

That there was trouble in the night
Is murmured and shrugged off:
There's no-one with the name for it,
The one right word that measures you
Hung by your shirt-sleeve in the cell

Like a sheaf of drying flowers,
A few spilled petals on the floor below.
They've murdered language, killed the one
Whose speech might act as searchlight through
The coagulating dark,

And name the action, name the act.
It's a big country with spaces on the map
And so many things to fill it with,
While the ants are placing grain on grain
In the circles of white ash.

THE LOOTERS

The helicopter cameras
Bring us the freeze frames.
A black sea outlines each peninsula
As snow finer than marble dust
Blurs the steeples of the spruce.
Bad weather, the wisdom goes.
Brings a community together.
Tonight the screen is a mirror
And the news is us.

At a house in Bedlinog
A drift has left its stain
Like a river in flood
Against the highest eaves.
There will be a plaque placed there soon
As if for some famous son,
While the cataract at Cwm Nash
Is a thirty foot long stalactite
Full of eyes and mouths
And the dazzling short circuits
Of a pillar of mercury.
An icicle uncirclable by three men.

Abandoned on the motorway
The container lorries are dislocated
Vertebrae. The freeze has broken
The back of our commerce
While on the farms, the snow-sieged
Estates, people return
To old technologies.

Meat is hung in double rows,
The carcasses identified
By the slashing beams.
Each one looms hugely,
Puzzling as a chrysalis
Under its silver condom of frost.
They sway like garments on a rack
When padlocks break and the freezer-
Doors swing out. It is too cold
Here to trail blood, where bread
Is frozen into breeze-blocks
And ten thousand tubes of lager
Sparkle under their ripping caul.
As flashlights zigzag up the wall
Tights turn red and tropical bronze
In each thin wallet.

The stranded drivers sleep in schools,
Their groups determined to uphold
The constitution of the snow.
Families smile through thermos-steam,
A child with her kitten, blue
As a cinder, sucking a blanket:
The usual cast of winter's news
As the commentary runs its snowplough
Through the annihilating white.

Outside, the cars are scoops
Of cumulus, and toboggans
Polish gutters in the drifts.
We never see the looters.

They move somewhere in the darkness
Through the blizzard, beyond the thin
Bright crescent of the screen,
Those people who have understood the weather
And make tomorrow's news.

YOPS

It waits for them
In the shadow, the rainsmoke.
The pines' blue quills
Sweep over it, and roof pitch
Blinks with all its lizards' eyes.
Then daylight turns its huge key
In the lock.

The shed fills up with fizzing smells and words.

The tabletop's burnt with their names
For each other, the scorched identities
Of this year's clutch of teenaged working men

Kicking the clodges round
In parched boots bracketed with lime
And studs like quillets, their brutal jewellery.
Through denim shreds move the cartoons
Of last year's loves and hates.

Over picks and mattocks
They push inside.
Over green cement dust frozen into ribs across the floor
They warm themselves on language hot as rum.

Wait an hour.
Feel the moods erupt, dissolve. Twitching
Like lurchers they face a world framed by a door
And walls where girls are starfish,
Sulky eels.

Low as rainsmoke, thermos-steam
The great frustrations hang.
Steelies start to tap the leaking boards.

DEVELOPMENT AREA

The chimneys work all shifts,
Flying their pennants of flame.
And where technicians crash
A ball about, the corals
Are a jumbled alphabet
In the tar.

At Crymlyn the prehistoric
Debris works out of the soil
Its monument to amnesia:
Plastics and metal and fine
Blue polythene
Like the wrappings of a city.

It's a territory of sirens;
But step behind the lorry park
And sulphur falls with the dew,
While down the glossy bark
Of the birches runs lichen
Like a lipsticked kiss.

Offices are hourglasses,
Secretaries their grains of sand.
On the glacier of the city's
Rubbish the children pick
For futures already discarded.
There is light here, but no window.

LEAVING MOZART TERRACE

He kept the taxi engine running,
Its exhaust dividing the valley
Like cellotape over a photograph.
The borrowed cases without addresses
Were heaved into the boot
By that boy with a black stub
Of moustache, his wrinkled cigarette
Thin as a straw.

I never imagined anywhere else.
By the path the bracken had been
Trampled into orange dust,
In the gutter the wheel-ironed cans
Were flattened like coins,
And all the takeaway rubbish,
Snowy, votive, streamed from the railings.
There was one man could remember
As far back as 1966
When Pink Floyd played the Non-Political.
He has the poster still,
Its powerful gothic in his school folder.

Going was easy.
There was something I was supposed to feel
But the boy drove as if he was late for something
And then through the rainglaze
Came the interchange with its sheaf of roads
And all the saplings snapped off in their concrete bowls.
Places can't be good or bad. They're just there.
We hardly had the chance to look round.

SUNGLASSES

(On the visit of Mrs Margaret Thatcher to Porthcawl, June 21, 1986)

We come to watch and to wait:
Perhaps to shout. Twenty people
On the promenade, an arc of the sea
Behind us, and a police dog in streaming
Gold fording a rock pool.

At my shoulder a small pressure:
A man in a grey suit
And sunglasses, his red crewcut
Like a saucer of iron filings.

Above us the legs of the police
Are screwed into stone;
Strangers on the roofs squint
Through lenses, their cameras
Feeding on our shadows.

And suddenly our chorus is blowing away.
I can examine my voice
As if it was a creature washed from the sea.
Then someone waves and the black
Limousines have disappeared.

In the restaurant we queue for takeaways.
Hello, says a voice. You're finished now?
The aluminium foil
Is like a mirror in his hands,
A bead of sweat on every thorn of his hair.
Then he puts on his sunglasses
And rubs out his face.

'WHAT'S THE POINT OF BEING TIMID WHEN THE HOUSE IS FALLING DOWN?'

Rumour, like blood, must circulate.
In movement it renews itself.

It was bleak, you said.
Wales was on the dole, and nobody cared;

The poets were in the traps
Waiting for the hare to come back;

In the country of the apathetic
The half-hearted man is king.

The fescue bleached, and the spiked bobbins of the teazle
Tip back and forth to the wind's pulse.

You had just made out
A staggering travel-expenses claim:

Train and bus I know give no free rides,
But John, I was driving you home.

For some reason I am digging,
Bruising my heel on the spade's blue shoulder.

And, creature of the great indoors,
It was strange that I should see you last

Walking up the Merthyr Road,
That ravaged sheepskin an affront to Whitchurch decency.

Six inches down I unearth a seam of frost,
Pale as anteggs, running into the dark.

Four in the morning is no time
To rediscover a savage malt:

The barman in pyjamas stared in weary disbelief;
Then turned, found the optics, and pressed.

It's all around me I suppose,
The invisible life of late winter

Accelerating now, an unstoppable rumour.
About you, famous drinkers,

Earnest lyric souls, and the merely loud
Had turned to wax.

There's something here that's at its end,
And something already edging into its place.

Make it a double, you grinned,
Savouring reunion with the Gaelic smoke.

The magpies in the hawthorn repair their dome,
In the barrels ice shrinks to a small dark embryo.

After all, a Sunday in Llandrindod
Offers no mercy to the squeamish.

THE HOT-HOUSE

1

Madness:
To be utterly
Without humour.

I watch obsession
Narrowing the grey
Meniscus of your eye.

This year the first you do not note
That hour of frosty spring
When the oak spurns its leaves

And they lie
Like brickred pheasant down
After a kill.

2

Evenings were spent around the hearth
Examining the anthology of flames.

See what you will in the orange
Honeycomb the coals become,

Every year the yuckers still fall
Down the spiral of the smoke,

Starlings tipped from the nest's wild raft
To catch a moment on the hooks of flame,

Their throats' yellow triangles
Part of the fire, opened as if for food,

Before flesh becomes bracken,
The skeletons of leaves,

The ghosts of flowers
In your abandoned books.

3

Today we walk in the rainforest
Under its hangar of glass.

There is a device there now,
An electric clock whose numbers

Spin remorselessly. Time is
Burning backwards towards zero

As the forest shrinks in front of us,
An acre destroyed every second.

This leaflet in my hand
Might be all our biographies.

It tells of species that become extinct
Before they are discovered.

4

Padlocks snap on the harvest,
Small flames run relays
Down the stubble lines.
This afternoon is hot and moist
As a coin held in the fist.

At three o'clock the curtains
Drawn, the electric fire's
Single bar a humming
Artery inside the room.
The t.v. whispers its conspiracies.

You stir the sugar through
Your tea but hardly touch its sweet
Mortar, as one by one
The noises of the street
Send you erect and shivering to the glass.

There's no-one there.
There never is. Only the roses
Tapping with their thorns the other
Side of the pane, and my own voice
Stirring, stirred

To nothing in the unbearable room.
Then I touch your dress
And all its electricity
Meets me like a blow.
Your sweat's the frosty scum of exhaustion.

There's nothing that can warm
You here. I've never felt
A skin so cold, a grip so tight.
And I leave you now
Spinning like a petal in a web.

5

In this part of the forest
All the creatures are unique.

Here is a woman
With nine rings on her fingers
And wine a garnet in her cup.

Her voice is like a tape
Played backwards, her mouth becoming
A black spool of words.

She points about her through the ward
At the jaguar's sulphuric
Eye, the webs of rain
That shiver in the treeferns.

We want to destroy them
Before we have understood.
It's fear of their strangeness
That lifts the weapons in our hands.

6

We come down from the upstairs ward
On the fire-escape's spiral.
Wolf-spiders hang their scaffolding
About us like a mist,
The wasps corkscrew
Through troughs of fallen fruit.

Behind the wall the garden has
Recovered its freedom.
Only us today on a morning walk
And a gang of boys beneath the chestnut trees,
White legs flashing through nettles
And the nettles' yellow stems

Hollow as hypodermics,
Splintering underfoot.
I think of the apples by your bed,
Their pale green pyramid untouched:
This year is turning profligate,
Its elderberries faded

To dull newsprint, the chestnuts
Only milky embryos
The boys have burst too soon.
Something I have to say, you said,
And I wait for the words that don't exist
That will pick this lock of grief.

Halfway down the tall staircase,
Its iron hoops like dinosaur bones,
You look around as if surprised
To see how far we've come.
There's a step towards me and a step away:
You're waiting there to choose.

7

Mornings and evenings
The same nurse lets us in.
He's worked a week of doublers,
Earning the authority
Of exhaustion, that mauve
Rim of the eye, the slight
Amused detachment
Of someone who has stopped
Testing himself. He brings
A hoop of keys, big as a wreathwire,
From the television lounge.
After seventy-eight hours
He is letting you go.

8

When you come for the weekend
You bring eighteen pairs of shoes,

And speak, it is a proverb,
Of the green damsons behind the wall,

A tree's bitter pebbles
That a week later will be

Mauve-skinned nipples
Squeezed and rolled around the mouth.

Now the miraculous tablet
Clings to your tongue,

You take communion
Four times a day.

The white crystal dissolves
And its dust lightens your eye

As one poison meets another
And sets you moving again

Through the first day, the second,
A week. A phial of pills

Stands on the shelf; lighter than eggshell,
Bitter as green damsons.

9

Under glass the air grown succulent
With heat. Above us the belfries
Of hibiscus and palm, a dead
Dateleaf like wet cardboard.
From the trees' silkscreen
The colours cloud and run.

We hold our coats,
Perspire, and gaze around.
Here's a bush that stands its flowers as
A collection of fine porcelain,
A kind of moss with blooms like Saturn's rings.
The arrows point through steamy latitudes.

But no tropical switchboard
Of voices here. Only temperate lives
Confused by the architecture of the plants,
Stunning grotesques whose petals lie
Like gobs of paint, whose stems
Are freakish torsos, dark and oiled.

You trail your bag with other visitors.
There's no way into the dangerous feast.
The sexless bees rave in the air
Or force an entry at a dragon's throat.
We watch each gleaming sphincter
Squeezing shut.

Behind this glass
The city's clocks,
The looks of those who might have
Ventured in, but would not
Change their stride.
So you make your way

Down the aisles of the rainforest,
Its colours erupting
Out of the dark green patina
Of night, lost for now
In something stranger than yourself.
Like the undiscovered peoples of the world.

THE MANSION

The house stands as it always has,
Its windows tall above the lake
And grass cut almost to the yellow root.

Along the drive a whitelimed kerb
Follows a perfect crescent,
As if stone, like air or water, moved in waves.

My steps dissolve in gardens where
The acid rhododendron thrives,
Its flowers pink and white as naked dolls.

It always was a selfish tree,
Devouring the light, growing
Glossy and alone, the strong inheritor.

At the door they take my card
And a name in silver italics
Grants entry where I never thought to pass.

These hands laid gently on my arm
Disturb an earlier trespasser,
That child under the yew hedge

Who watched the long cars slide through his village
And women shaped like candleflames
Moving over the lawns.

Above his head the berries swelled
As soft as wax around each nucleus,
The black nugget of poison that would grow.

THE VERGER

Every day his bonfire
The shape of a tepee
Showed its reluctant smoke.

Springs through a mattress those thin coils,
The cut grass glowing like tobacco
As he fanned it with a sack.

Later I'd walk over to where
A thrush had smashed a tigerstriped snailshell
And the wires of a wreath

Lay like a burnt-out catherine-wheel.
Brambles covered the graves,
A ball of caterpillars pulsed in its silk nebula,

And there on the fire would lie
The bodies of snakes the verger had hunted
Through the cool, vitreous ivy of the hedge,

The harmless grass-adders he'd swung like flails
Against a piece of marble coping
In that vendetta he pursued

Daily and determinedly
Against the graveyard's secret life.
Perhaps he thought it exposed some mystery,

Leaving the grass-snakes there
With damp-scorched testaments
And dead hydrangea heads like dolls' wild hair.

Agate green and grey
Ran the traceries of grass-snake skin,
Their scissor-jaws agape.

Slowly the bonfire toppled
Like an angel into the weeds.

EPILOGUE

We bring you apples in a plastic bag
And build a pyramid of offerings
Around the radio. I feel its current,
Bloodlike, faint as breath.

It was hard to find the ward:
I remembered a railway siding
Where the coaches are stalled amongst
Scorching ragwort, and there is
One carriage with its windows broken
And a name sprayed down the side,
As if language is the last defiant act.

But you're not speaking
And we listen to ourselves fill drawers
With the words you don't require,
And all I can think of is you at dewfall,
The hem of your dress in a black hoop,
Plucking the sour champions from the trees
Where lichen is splashed orange
As yolk and hangs its tapers
Of goathair from the bark.

It's only the living that hold me here.
Your gaze goes further than that stubbled youth
With earrings like the silver
Wheels of a watch, holding flowers
And a ribboned box
That will never be untied;
And beyond these spruce-green orderlies

Smoothing out a bin-liner
As if a crease in a child's dress.
They are all too near, or new, for your concern.

But with them I form a circle
You cannot break. You're the stranger here
I will not recognise, a face
Empty as the misted water in this jug.
You've turned away from everything
That I could do or say,
So that there's nothing left to think about
But the yellow beads of applesap
I want to see about your mouth
Before we pack up, turn the channel off.

THE STONES THEMSELVES

Our children choose the life outside,
Needling the eyes of a pomegranate,
Making dens behind the bramble-curtained graves.

Death and devotion mean nothing
To their play, these tablets that we fail
To read flaking like birch-bark,

Notched with a language
Blurred as the scars of ivy on the church.
The stones themselves must know exhaustion here

And lean together like old men
In some hateful conspiracy.
An old man's evening, stone-dusk, drifts within the room.

And I would soon leave but for her
Wedged into a corner of the floor
That crackles with religious dust,

This globe-woman, squat as a pomegranate,
A grinning thalidomide shape
Holding herself hugely apart.

She smiles from her belly through the church
Offering us the honeycomb
Which these shrunken men refused to sip.

Unhistoried and unexplained
No coin in the charity box saves her.
I listen for her children in the dark.

FAIRGROUND MUSIC

1. Dawn

The mist comes out of Somerset
And the air turns to ash.
In the rain a man caresses
The beach with the slow
Arcs of a metal detector.
Every morning the pennies
And ruptured cans
Are moments of discovery
Exciting the dial.
But between the squill and the thrift
The single clue today
Is this fine blue plastic
Like the skin of some creature
Grown immense and moved away,
Leaving these fragments of identity.
Only its absence is making sense.

2. Wild Strawberries

The alsatian waits beside their bags
And gives you the family stare.
A golden muscle twitches in its neck.

Father's stopped and lies down in the ferns,
Blue roses on his forearms
And each elbow inked with spiderwebs.

The children gob the bitter hulls,
Whilst the youngest, rashed with sunburn,
Cries behind the blackened stones of their fire.

The mother's blind to all of this:
She fills a tiny handkerchief
As if she had to make up time on shift,

And into the bank pushes a face
White and pitted as the underside
Of a strawberry someone picked too soon.

3. Nuns Bathing

From the garden to the dunes
Laughter threads their single file.

Brown as fieldfares
They move towards the waves

And climb the sea-eaten wall
For the green pencils of samphire,

Smiling at something not of this place
And sniffing their lemony fingers.

Each one holds a camera.
Their children are already conceived.

4. *Double English*

When the inspector walked into the room
Mr Holt's eyes grew cloudy as lemonjuice.
He was giving out a poem by Walter de la Mare,
Still sooty from the photocopier
And warm in the hand.

Mr Holt taught in a girls' school
Because he liked boys.
Years ago in another place
He had taken two lads to the funfair
And they had all travelled upside down
On the Wheel of Fate.
The money had fallen out of Mr Holt's pockets,
But it was better than double English.

The inspector took a copy to the back seat.
He was a headquarters-type of person
In nescafé-coloured trousers.
Politeness left a cool space around him.
It was only a short poem,
And Mr Holt had found it in a very old book,
The one he always used for poetry lessons.

The ghost-train was hot and stuffy
As a wardrobe. A green face
Shone in the darkness like a luminous clock.
Mr Holt put his hand on the knee
Of one of the boys. He put out his hand
And there was screaming and laughter

And the echoes of laughter.
Then the doors banged open
And his headmaster was standing by the ticket-booth.

Reading the poem, Mr Holt listened to the echoes.
There were words in it
You never heard any more
And things that might be difficult to explain.
Mr Holt had never been much good at explanations.
The page was cold.
And glancing at the clock of the inspector's face
He noted there were exactly fifty-eight minutes to go.

5. Around the World

He gives you an end-of-season face,
Half exhaustion, half contempt.
But that is the face he always gives,
Dropping your coins into his purse
And pulling the lever in the booth.
The children ride a figure-of-eight
On a yellow plastic train.
Like him they stare out seriously
As they move past gorges, waterfalls
And a line of snowy peaks.
No-one ever comes back.

6. Ghost Train

A paperback novel
Placed cover up,
The headphones pulled down tight
Inside her hair.

No need to talk.
She pushes out tickets with the change
And we step into a carriage
On the rail.

Through the cracks in their fingers
Our children
Squint at oblivion.
The soundtrack's running down like a lit fuse.

And from her hutch of glass
This girl stares out,
The disc of tickets turning on its spike.
Her purple nails
Are filed like arrowheads.

7. In the Arcade

The money hangs over a precipice:
One nudge and it should fall.
Strange it never works like that
And soon the slots are jammed
And a man unlocking the sump of coins.

Forced to his knees he embraces it,
The silver, slippery money-child
That has leapt into his arms.
At their machines the gamblers pause,
Then look away from a private act.

8. Bronze Age

Fat and black
As a fern shaft's sickle root
It lies where I turned
Over that zinc sheet
I will never inch back into place.

Like these helleborines
Snake-lipped and -eyed,
Gleaming with nectar,
It fixes the gaze
With an old narcotic.

In the wreck of the dunes
It basks amongst tokens
Of all our squalid summers;
Its abandoned sleeve of skin
A broken spiderweb.

Only the voltage of fear
Keeps the current
Running between us.
And then I understand:
Through this litter-dappled park

The Bronze Age
Has sent an emissary:
Smudged ace of diamonds
On its neck, the hollow tooth
A tiny phial of delirium.

9. Madam Zeena

A breeze moves the plastic
Skirts of the hut
As she traces the palm's hieroglyphic.

Under the curtain
The feet of a fast-food queue,
The dabs of paint and effervescent rusts
On the Wheel of Fate.

And at her table
A fat schoolboy. nodding
And pink-freckled as an orchid,
Cheekbones rouged by sunlight
In the chalk of his face;

A lunchtime schoolboy
Awkward and shivering in the gloom,
As the mystery of what happens
Is confessed to him.

10. Fathers

Flat out amongst the towels
And empty flasks they lie
As their fathers might have done,
Eyes closed, not sleeping,
But for a time untouchable,
As if a line was drawn
Around them in the sand.

Their children play on a mat
Of restharrow, crinkly as a perm,
The radio's tuned to the tumult
Of contemporary lusts.
Along their shoulders' thickening yoke
Tattoos fade to a mockery
Of everything they thought they could predict.

11. The Track

The fairground has its neon midsummer.
There is a pavement of limestone
Beyond its edge, above the powerboats
That press like captured birds
Against the cage of the bay.

Listen, the voices of children spinning
On a ferris wheel, an irregular step
Down this three thousand year-old road
Of plastics and corals and the compass points
Of gentian leaves pricked out of chalk.

Away from the conflagration of light
A figure stumbles through the dunes,
And two hikers, upright crustaceans,
Follow the blistered families
Who drag their shopping through tall grass.

Now driftwood flares in its ring of stones
And a well of voices bubbles from the slope
Of Cog-y-brain. Two lovers, sullen
Amidst buckthorn, stare away from each other.
The neon cools in embers overhead.

12. From the Summit

As we fall and rise
On the Wheel of Fate
Our voices are peeled away.

Swinging us above the town
It holds us now an instant,
Breath frozen, upside down,
Staring outward at the roofs
Of cars and aisles of caravans,

Towards that profile of the dunes,
Their neolithic sunset
Through the blue buckthorn.

And distantly, as far as sight allows,
A figure on the beach
Is sweeping a crescent on the sand,
Someone alone, heartbreakingly small,
Who would make the great discovery.

Then machinery crashes
And the whole town's like a film reeled back
As we rush towards the ground.

A MAP OF THE SKY

The poplar's fleece floats to the ground
And moths are embers stirred
To one last flame. This is a night
Of meteorites, the stars flashing
Like silverfish out of the dark,

Whilst Venus is a bonfire on the ridge.
We have our glass and telescope
But rather trust our eyes for this
Performance of the century,
The fall of startling dust.

At last the curious leave, but you
Still pace a furrow in the lawn,
Tieing ribbons to the trees
And folding hands into a careful shell
That holds a voice of grief, your fierce laugh.

But I remember you, the usherette,
Leading me through the cinema's
Warren, a torchbeam's hot
Quiver of light brushing my face
As if it was your glove.

And later at the interval
Standing with your icy tray
As we blinked at the return
To ourselves. I could only marvel
At the calm smile on your face

As the children hopped to touch
Your neat theatre uniform
And the fathers shuffled foolishly
While they waited for their change.
In all that auditorium

When the stuffy wardrobe darkness fell
You were the one who glided through
Untouched by our confusion,
A line of quicksilver in your hair
From the projection room's white pane.

Now the names of your enemies
Are spelled in coloured porcelain
Along the mantelpiece, in plastic
Flowers potted in the hall.
The garments on a washing-line

Are the silhouettes of all your torturers.
Under these trees you seem to fill
With the domestic anger of the world,
Every terror, tyranny
Become the yellow eyes of china dogs,

The thwarted energies of quiet streets
Directing your voice
Out of the garden, up toward
The neighbours' conspiratorial
Lines of pink lampshades.

You are out there crying in the dark,
Hurting with language and the deaths
Of mayflies, fallen meteors,
As we pull our curtains, draw the blinds
Like a cloud across the sky.

STAFF

I

Her day-long smile
Welcomes you to the building.
She is money's
Immaculate reflection.

II

The morning ritual
Is to take a steel ruler
And slash her way through envelopes
That do not bear her name.

III

Every minute she connects
One voice to another,
Letting them play
Around each other like finches.
She is the cage.

IV

She hangs the smell of pine-
Forests over enamel,
Plots the orbits of the polisher.
All those nameless good-evenings
Might echo forever
As she flicks on lights in empty corridors,

V

At five in the November dusk
Here is the sum of her day's work,
A corn-coloured sheaf of envelopes
Forgotten long before it's sent
Sliding through the dark.

VI

You remember her from school,
Third form, fourth, a mind
That threatened even then
To fit this flax-blue uniform.
Already there lolls about her face
Compliant middle age,
All the ancestry of discos
And white bread. Her hands
In taking up your purchases
Tap out a brief sonata.

VII

The desks are put back into line,
A paper with one grey
Footprint swept up.
From the corner there is last retrieved
A broken piece of chalk.
If the board was clean
What would she write?

VIII

Newspaper, sandwich, radio.
She waits with the others
In the revving taxi rank:
As the train pulls out, its passengers
Run to ticketed cars;
And soon the diesel's fainter than the breath
Of her children crumpled
Into balls of sleep.

MEN

In the cool Jersey air
The Buicks are nose to tail
On the highway and their horns
Calling to each other like owls.

And the men sit and
Wait, elbows on the rolled-
Down glass, the clockfaces
In the dash starting to glow.
The dusk turns petrol-blue.

They look at the backs
Of each other's heads
As the Boeings go over
With burning lights
And the silver Amtrack carriages
Knife past without a breath.

They stare at each other's
Bristling scalps, the pugnacious
Shaping of a skull,
Seeking out a statement there,
Measuring the distances.
And ahead a horizon
Of refineries, the neon
Signature of Miller's Lite.

SKETCHES OF MAY

1

I make my daughter restless
With images of you,
Dreaming your face in cracked plaster,
A pattern of the dust.

Easier now in this absolving light
To smile at skin like bruised oranges,
Hair a bonfire's smoke,
As you lash me with an eye's ferocious squint.

Virginity, our village
And all the world's amnesia
Have shrivelled you like a bible-primrose.
You nurse your dolls in cindered lanes

And here pause breathless on the hill
Until traffic startles you
Like a moth out of the grass
Back to your kitchen.

I think of mealtimes
And the schoolgirl words of grace
Over a single plate wide as a scream,
Your eyes' violet needlepoints

As the light in the cottage
Is scrabbled off and your face
Turns to the dark, while a child
Demands a story that will scare.

You sit on a ledge in the malthouse
Looking down the road
And your petticoat is like a thumbed *Echo*.

In your hands the stone face,
Fist-sized gargoyle you dug
Out of the frost, between the ash-path

And the red nipples of rhubarb.
That notched image you brought straight to us
Like a child carrying a butterfly,

A thin, piratical face,
Dark outline tracing its sneer
Even after we had scrubbed it under the hot tap.

"There", we said. And laughed at the mannikin.
But peered closer, suggesting
Periods of history like authors' names.

Now you curl over the sill,
Knees pressed together shiny as spectacles,
While in your hands the creature smiles —

A little demon, genius of the village —
And slowly we grow envious
Of what you will never surrender.

THE SUNSTROKE SONNETS

1

Crickets in the scrub,
The virgins at their prehistoric chant.
In the face of the cliff
A fossil's stopped clock.

My head swims. Seen enough.
The body with its rough garment
Turns aside as the light
Follows to a garden

Of hibiscus and blue
Bees. And when the pains approach
They are curious strangers,
Or the slow, heraldic
Bugs marching through thyme.

2

Madonna of thorns:
Each leaf a pinion.

Drawn by this the blood leaps
But her garment is untouchable.
The hand cannot travel with the eye.

At every footfall
Beetles scatter like dice,
The smooth obsidian, dark as sunglasses,

Glares from the path.
I would trace the milk of her throat,
The mauve and ivory of her dress.

Three times I circle like the dust
Or the hooded crows in their spiral.
But the woman of thorns gives no approach.

3

This is a bad mirror.
It shows someone who is not myself
Vague and pulsing in its chrysalis.

Go out. A man draws a net
From the bay, the fish stretched
Like an alphabet over its staves.

In the bars language and music
Make a space for themselves.
White walls; black coffee:
Across the air the mosquitoes' barbed wire.

So a dish of bread, the parching wine,
And the rubbish falls a thousand feet,
Tins and fire and polythene
Over the island into the sea.

AFTER BREAKFAST

1

Battle Creek, Michigan, USA,
Says the name on the cereal packet,
Which is where Jesus Christ might live today

Filling your bowl with sunshine.
But you think about a beaten tribe
Ambushed at the ford, all bloody-headed

As the woodpecker outside,
Whose language knows no vowels,
Whose yellow feathers sometimes glow in your wardrobe,

A remnant shrinking out of history.
Rinsing your cup at exactly
Nine o'clock you can measure what survives.

2

The dress trembled like the hot ring's
Violet cones of gas. You had never touched
Anything softer, even in the moist heart

Of the mangolia that the petals concealed.
But the man's hand hardly traced
Your breast, that other secret place,

Before your mother spoke without vowels
From the edge of the plantation,
And you ran home sucking a nettle blister.

In the morning the dress hung in ribbons
Above the garden; three magpie tails
Fluttering from the clothesline. Outlaws.

3

Every August under bricks and glass
The marrow, like a smooth
Green child, would trail its cord,

And the swallows in the shed leave their hard
Adobe cups for the telegraph lines,
Voiceless themselves as electricity.

Into the ledger you printed
Holiday rotas, a listing of pick-ups,
Put-downs and maintenance chores

For a village transport company.
Soon, more than county-wide your lorries,
Smooth and green, were bearing your legend.

4

Outside the snow grew thicker than the common's
Cottongrass. That hill was almost
One in five, and the only wiper's pendulum

Starting to drag. But not the slightest fear
As you skidded into the bwlch
On a low-gear route back to the books.

Afterwards, your pencil traced icicles
Down page after page while winter passed,
But high in the cab on a mountain road,

The engine ecstatic under your foot,
The great simplicities of wood and stone
Were a load delivered and delivering.

5

Most Fridays you would step from the salon,
Too tight, too pigeon-coloured,
And the usual taxi take you home.

On the kitchen shelf huddled a platoon
Of seven silverfoil-necked bottles,
A line of white chessman that never moved.

You understood that one touch meant
You played until the end. Coming in
And flicking dust from their shoulders,

You checked the tops were absolutely sealed.
And sometimes thought about the cloud
Writhing slowly through the jubilee beer.

6

There's an archaeology of piston-
Rings in the long grass, postcards in a drawer.
All that you've learned from waiting gives them sense.

Living begins, you said, when you can stop
Wondering when something will happen.
Rinsing your cup at nine o'clock, taking

The unburnt log out of the grate —
Its crown of sparks redder than the woodpecker —
You settle yourself in silence on the chair

Your mother used, the straightbacked vehicle
That is carrying you through time.
Now face to the wall you feel the hurricane.

A FOOTNOTE TO THE HISTORY OF BRIDGEND

In a cellar up the lane
The future is about to happen.
A boy opens his fist
And the mauve tablet lies there
Like a pinch on his skin.
He grows as pale as elderwood.

Guitars come out of the vans
And all the unrecognisable
Schoolgirls line themselves against
The walls, a different insignia
At their throats, eyes sooty
As the shy, tree-hurdling lemur's.

They hug each branch of chill
Brickwork as Pink Floyd stir
The cauldron. I am on the hill
Behind the yellow eldertrees
Watching the birth of 1966.
This might be anywhere, say the cynics;

The fact that it is not
Will only occur to me
When it is too late, ours never being
A precocious country.
Meanwhile in the nextdoor barber's shop
Instruments tremble on glass shelves.

BOTANY

All I know is, we were there together,
Perhaps for the last time.
The chase ended, and you in red sandals,
Ankles cut by the pipes of the stubble,
And the dog flung down in the restharrow,
A lace of spittle on his tongue.
Below us lay the hot limestone
Of the field's incline, and above,
A magpie's flight blurred like a dice
That rolls unreachably away.

You are still there, with your sunburn
Darker than a ladybird,
And on a pillar of the coconut-smelling gorse
A stonechat, piercing with
Its song the cushions of the air.
Years later I come back
With a camera and crouch down
Under the thorn, pushing the blue
Bead of the lens towards
The orchid that grows in the place where you lay.

ISOLATION WARD

The hypodermic is big
As a bicycle pump.
She slips the blade
Between blue vertebrae
And I count in a language
I have never learned
Until it is released.

I grow thin and polished
As the rim of a wheel,
Squeezing the delirious
Animals out of my mind
To make the audience gasp —
Sad relatives erect
In their uniforms of flowers.

No-one touches me but her
Whose duty is each day
To take the hot stones from my head
And stroke me with the irises
Picked on the moor, transparent
Webs of ice the last petals,
Green bottles of a dangerous seed.

Then she whispers far into my sleep
Teaching me to walk.
My cheek's upon the silver
Eye of her watch, face clenched
In her groin. Behind glass
The children are like thistledown
She is blowing towards home.

IN THE WATCHTOWER

The frontier hums, a live
Cable carrying our charge.
Barbed wire and the sentry posts
Bristle against a wall of acid firs:
Climbing the steps I'm brushing off
Their needles hooked into my clothes,
The needle wax's scent of oranges.

It's safe here in the clock-tower —
The villagers' dovecote —
Where sunlight varnishes the boards
And soldiers lean their guns
Against a wall, put down
Binoculars and take to twisting round,
Like farmers with a barren hen,
The necks of tall bottles.

And I smile as they step, dainty as girls,
Out of the rifles' harnesses,
Thinking of my grandfather
And the scornful way he'd leave his spade
After a morning's couch-cutting,
Relief flexing through the racked
Sinews, yellower than iris roots,
And spreading from the halfmoons of his sweat.

I've never seen a gun so close,
This grey snub-barrelled thing
Shining like a beetle's carapace,
No bigger than a toy's image.
But touching it might set the bells

Above us, now a cluster of blue grapes,
Speaking the first syllables
Of the last war, and loose the doves —
Preening on the shoulders of bellmetal —
In a volley over Czechoslovakia.

Those fields swim in a blue-green haze
Like the pages of a passport.
I stop, and feel the current stir
Beneath me, two armies praying
To the eager god of electricity,
While a family of leverets
Wild as pinball in the grass
Cross frontiers within sight but out of range.

CONE JELLIES

Behind us the pylon crackles
As we tread a hollow of cold
Sand. Electricity mutters
In its hive, over the dagger-grass,
Over the wayfarer tree, embraced
By a tribe of green crickets,
Their ancient faces set
All as one away from the sea.

Out on the waves the cone-
Jellies shine in the darkness
Like confetti on a wet road;
Each creature a flake of mirror-silver.
I think of the surprising child
Lodging now within you,
One of those stray bullets of mercury
That has passed from the evening tide.

You and your first man created this.
In the sand we touch a fern's
Velvety antlers, the nuggets of coral
From our resort's tropical past.
It might look like these, your daughter, your son;
We are giving it a shape with words;
Already it has a history,
Whilst all this frightened laughter makes it huge.

For a mile your lover walks
With us. His hair is red and trembles
Like the sea-anemones, his accent
Sharp as salt from the exploding wrack.

But he is fading with the far coastline,
Shrinking as the child grows up.
Soon his music and his hot whiskey
Are the empty shells of anecdote.

Today I climb the stairway
Past every ruined floor, hearing
The dancers practice, young men
In ragged vests who shout routines,
Plimsolls beating to smoke
The ceiling's fallen plaster.
Leaving behind the last stone flight, yours
Is the landing without a bannister.

The coffee's made in soup-bowls
And you stir in honey
Carefully as paint, watching the liquid
Thicken. In quilted jacket,
Feathery breath, you lean the paintings
On the walls, asking what I see.
And I stand before the canvasses
Like a child at a forest edge.

In this studio the sky
Is one small pane. Stepping through
The trap-door on to the city's roofs
I touch the corbels curled
Like knuckles, the chimneys glazed
And corpulent in a congregation
Above the street. But here I'm in retreat,
Fearful of the figures crouched

In the scintillating midnights
Of your oils, their besieged zones of light.
There's nothing I can recognise
For these are places words don't go.
I would have this in my house, I say,
Wondering how I might live with such questioning.
On the table a quiver of brushes soaks
In water the colour of blood.

Now we edge into the dockland club
And the doorman shuts us in.
This is the triumphal afterworld
Of copper-tables, pumice-rough,
And a fire in its small temple
Leaping from a dark eyelet of gas.
Here there are no orders called
And the clocks have turned to stone.

Your skin is dirty-pale as old
Piano keys. One day out
Of hospital you have scoured yourself
As we read that artists must,
Made the thrilling choice and brushed aside
All meagre interference.
So you smile and roll a cigarette
Already crushed like one of your tubes of paint.

A city mapped with dolls' eyes,
The Da-Da bowler-hat. Such newborn
Studio images we toured before our drink.
I felt textures built by pallet-knives,

Their daubs and slashes creating
The ruthless marriage of your oils.
We all believe we have the right
To paint out our mistakes.

I watch a woman approaching
Who takes our empty bottle from the ledge,
Slim-shouldered, scarved with silver foil,
And rolls it to oblivion.
You're returning to the attic-space
And the smeared board that waits
On its cradle, the figures only
Pencilled ghosts to whom you're bringing life.

LOOKING FOR ARTHUR

Now here was a valley stranger than most
In the legends. A heap of rusted cars
Lay racked like toast, and the pool of green
Nitrogen simmered between rocks.

We expected distant shouts,
Some land-manager's pursuit of our trespassing,
But only the silence accosted us
As we moved under the wall of the engine-house,

Higher, it seemed, than a cathedral,
Its gorgeous brickwork prickly with red moss,
And left the known world behind.
The mountain wore a scarf of mist

And below us now the buzzard
Floated like a fallen handkerchief.
I climbed in silence, middle-aged respect,
But the children creased the solemn tarns

With handfulls of the scree, dragging
Wellies through those cauldrons in the peat.
They swung on ropes of voices to the crown,
To discover that we were explorers

Of what someone else already knew,
But to retrieve from the cave's maw
This one horseshoe, whose rusting leaves
As yew-wood does, a regal dust

Against the skin, and glimpse the ocean's
Pale eyelid winking in its notch,
While at our feet a hare lay pressed
As flat as ruined corn.

Acknowledgements

Some of these poems have appeared in the following magazines: *Ambit, The Green Book, Planet, Poetry Wales, New Welsh Review, Verse, 2 Plus 2, Rural Wales.* Others have been published in the anthologies *Glas Nos* (CND Cymru) and *The Poetry Book Society Anthology 1987-88* (Hutchinson) and have been broadcast on *Poetry Now* (Radio 3).